Golden Satellite Debris

Also by Martin Corless-Smith

Poetry
The Melancholy of Anatomy (Shearsman Books 2021)
The Fool & The Bee (Shearsman Books 2019)
Bitter Green (Fence Books 2015)
English Fragments: A Brief History of the Soul (Fence Books 2010)
Swallows (Fence Books 2006)
Nota (Fence Books 2003)
Complete Travels (West House Books 2000)
Of Piscator (University of Georgia Press 1998)

Prose / Essays
The Poet's Tomb (Parlor Press 2020)
The ongoing mystery of the disappearing self (SplitLevel Texts 2020)
This Fatal Looking Glass (SplitLevel Texts 2015)

Translations
Odious Horizons: Some Versions of Horace (Miami University Press 2019)

Martin Corless-Smith

Golden Satellite Debris

Shearsman Books

First published in the United Kingdom in 2024 by
Shearsman Books Ltd
PO Box 4239
Swindon
SN3 9FN

Shearsman Books Ltd Registered Office
30–31 St. James Place, Mangotsfield, Bristol BS16 9JB
(this address not for correspondence)

www.shearsman.com

ISBN 978-1-84861-948-7

Copyright © Martin Corless-Smith, 2024.

The right of Martin Corless-Smith to be identified as the author of this work has been asserted by him in accordance with the Copyrights, Designs and Patents Act of 1988.
All rights reserved.

ACKNOWLEDGEMENTS

None of these poems have appeared elsewhere. I would like to thank those that have read versions of this manuscript and offered me advice and encouragement. Thanks to Alan Halsey and Kelvin Corcoran; Forrest Gander and Cole Swensen; Dan Beachy-Quick and Peter Gizzi. Thanks most recently to Chris V. Eaton and Sara Nicholson.

And to Wendy, for everything.

Contents

I.	Fludd Street	9
II.	Golden Satellite Debris	37
III.	The Erstwhile Gods	59
IV.	The Red Book	93
V.	In a Foreign Field	99

Afterword   120

The fairest universe is but a heap of rubbish piled up at random.

—Heraclitus

gods ruin the day with ecstasy
so I am sick with worry
and the floating lights that play
above the estuary

Fludd Street

Sweet mad regal river
rising to our upper floor

The Tyburn crosses under Wigmore St.
an elevation notable
(Uchida's Schubert
sonata no. 21)
a dip on Piccadilly
entering Green Park
making then its confluence
with Mother Thames.

The Epicenes

Taking the nightbus
N9, N10, N11
The madrigal
Epicenes
lounge in phosphorescent
Heaven
legs dressed in ambiguous sheen
Light green gowns
surrounded by
reflections of
the same scene
projected onto
floating night
out the window
down below
the driver hums
a dream in
deep vermilion
the sleeping workers
returning home
repeat
end-of-the-line
sleep unaware
of an open floor
above them
where angels
in exchange for safety
dare

The view from William Williamson's balcony, Fludd Street, SW1

On the sacred second floor
in a house that can't exist
Following the ringing call
a narrow footpath through the hall
singing now is not allowed
singing is no longer heard
where are we to gather in our hope
tiny ash fragments lift up
nobody has a reason to
the oasis is a desert now
trees became stumps
stumps powder
powder fuel
the crown floats in vinegar
the crown ruins the whole
ruins the small and mighty
in one go.
All those people William
that have died
all those people William loved
lying in their yards
waiting to be lowered in a hole
given up into the atmosphere
bending like a meteor off course
yesterday and yesterday
when we all lived thoughtlessly
with memories and futures and besides
that more importantly
the ignorance of every day
a stranger walking down our road
should know we have closed up
the houses frozen in their glares

the dogs worn out their barks
collapsed in collapsed yards
the attic windows blasted out
by bombs the steeple
lying docile in the park.
No hope will ever come to you
no word of joy be heard outside
out loud the crowd has dwindled
past the spectacle of no one being left alive.

Gabriel

The girl-boy whistles from
On high a tune at once
Familiar and faintly off
Almost like a memory
Or something not yet set
Yet recognizable we
Hardly notice that we do
Our busy lives
In terminals
As destinations
Or transitional
Gabriel
Bringer of messages
And light ambiguous
We thought we needed
Absolute authority
Riding in particular
Carriages and carousels
Listening to orchestra-ted
Parables exercising
Judgement and our bodies
Working out to hope
It all works out
Where in the world is time enough
To improvise a whistle
Draped flamboyantly
To shock our children
Into laughter verging
On fear verging
On ecstasy verging
On the Virgin weeping at the news

Christ's Entry into Brussels, 2022

The priest must not lead us astray. In the beginning the priest and the poet were one—only later ages separated them.
       —Novalis, *Philosophical Writings*

I'm ovulating
not like that
insane asylum
invitations
discount code
you could push
a blade into my neck
because you disagree
with me. An idea
resulting in an act
I'm menstruating
not like that
the women chase me
down the hall
cheering with
the noise of static
eyes uncanny
dreaming of Ophelia
and Tuscany
I'm giving birth
I hardly meant to
but the long & short
of it is that I
had no choice
free will being as it is
I've miscarried
maybe I'm your criminal
crossing from one state
into another

I've aborted
you're my daughter
and the shop is shut
who said anyone should know
it's a disgrace
the state of grace these days
heaven knows these Christians
are fundamentally obscene
you can't even suck a cock
without some asshole
charging you a fee
and when Christ comes again
to town dressed in a lady's gown
all glittery with makeup on
imagine their surprise when
they don't get an invitation
to the party lacking
the imagination
and appropriate attire.

Waking fantasia with gods

My jubilee, in both worlds Zeus
Of word and deed entwined
Pure gold from the commingling of thighs
He can maintain at night his high reception
Through patterned cosmic maps
Arrays infernal drive him to his undone
Mortal and immortal lust
In fear and anger she transforms
Her beauty forced into disgust
No challenge to his hasty guise
His mask and bill the schwanen delves
He must because he must
A stranger entering the house
Esteems the sacrifice and raises
Oceanus in his liquid coils.
Invisible Hephaestus wraps
Infinitesimal gold
Around us in a net
As vital and precise
As time and consequences
Gods may cease and gods may quake
But no one doubts the unrelenting foil

Water music

Villa d'Este's water courses
I can hear a song
I can hear a song begin
As we enter Ippolito's park

Oh frank celestial love
The woods are wild and magical
A stranger meets you on the path
And takes away your captive soul

The water spouts most playfully
Outrageously powered dalliance
The cascade comes from miles away
From mountains we can barely see

August augury

Now is my time on earth
confined by rising floods
here in my quartered yard
the mower stalled

M. reduced to this
hiding in plain sight
sergeants in squad cars
underneath flood lights

Who voiced these useless prophecies
that carry emptiness as if it mattered
desperation gathered greedily
by witnesses both resolute and blind

I find a broken microscope
hidden in a desktop drawer
in the guest house room I rent
travelling abroad

I rig the lens so I can see
sugar crystals on a slide
glow like icebergs in the night
interstellar satellites

I'm not frightened for the world
a dragonfly has landed on a peach
I have nothing to offer anyone
the ocean answered by a floating leaf.

May augury

The endless bubos frolick in my crease
equipment late in coming and defunct
I'll whimper with my aniseed and rum
sat with a view over collapsing Christendom

When the real bard was born
half his town was riven down
still he plucked a goose quill pen
to mate the muse and quarry men

Rose gold morning
aqua night
the ghost of cities
whisper through the trees

We lived in silence
crumpled cars in stacks
along the empty freeway
where the gators sun

Carrying nosegays in their beaks
every workshop idle, empty streets
sound from every quarter ceased
only music rising from invisible retreats

I hear the flowers die
the doors and windows blink
maws swallow sound
sparrows peck the ground inaudibly

A bleach spot on the map
increases like the sun at noon
until we can no longer see
the place we thought we once belonged

Lifts up her skirt
to piss into the gutter
of the empty street
and walks toward the square

Remember when we met here
when the college used to meet
and students sat with confidence
around the fountain seat

And there were pigeons
we ignored and sparrows
under chairs and sandwiches
we shared just over there

The automated bells chime three
which means it is the afternoon
which means it's almost time
to go back home

Past the nameless stretches
of standing water
and the undistinguished
twigs of endless shrubs

Past the outskirts
of the urban stains
the tree-lined littered parks
the small contained play areas

Past the leaning hoardings
with the out-of-date advert
the once-compelling face
static in a mute announcement

Shop after shop
car after car
the weeds entwining
lamppost and insignia

Here in a city once
reportedly
the centre
of the great empire

Here on the hard
shoulder with the
radio
static panicking

Metallic wheezing
of the green finch
of the dormant crane
the rusty swing

The green finch isn't really green
it's more a local blend of mousy grey
and smudgy faded gold
its beak a beige pink twig

The crane so high it seems to almost lean
over its evacuated site
Lilly-narcissus by his pond,
the playground swing swings intermittently.

*

It hurts me to look
at the house where you lived
I can't be sure
if it's my death or yours

And is it art?
brought back to life
a knowledge peeled
from my eye skin

All that we hurt and bear
makes nothing that will last more than an hour

From the wild woods we hide
grow figs, grow dates, grow obsolete inside

Bredon Hill in the time of the Corona Plague

Seen from the bluff
Malvern is a lavender blue cuff
Turned against the evening clouds
Last waft of warm fading to high blown grey
We cannot see the streets with shuttered doors
Nor any isolating home or boarded shop
Only a haze of settling dusk
The green of where we stand
Is losing out its sap to cold
No one is about, no car lights in the vale
Towns sit oddly mute, off season
Full and empty like old orchards
Of abandoned fruit.
With the last of the sun
We must head back
To try and put this all together
Into one sustaining thought
A world continuing beyond
The limit of our lonely view.

April augury

Easter weekend the flood has risen
Past the approximate prediction
With uncertain consequences
The brown slurry fingers through the fences

Here is the poem I was given
for an audience concerned
with drowning in the river
risen up their basement stairs

Here is the answer I have
for the poorly prepared heaven
our underground demons
flooding hidden graves

Overhead drone
of invisible plane
having tools
but not a plan

Numbers out do us
each love story
loss of virginity
flushed into obscurity

It's funny to think
that reading the famous
once brought us closer
to history's chapter

Possibly sane certainly sinking
As we eat canned soup and
Finding little reasons
To carry on

The poet never has a house

A general may invade the land

A pathogen or some insult

The neighbour birds fly off

Before a warning shot is even fired

I have renounced this sofa,
cup, even this tea
you cannot steal a dime
from this short rhyme

The army turns left
over the bridge
breath foggy
in their masks

The town is empty
reeks
of sweat
& entropy

the pets know how to die
at their masters' feet
the deer know the instant when
the streets are empty

*

returning to box
just what you need
what would you save
for the next world

Earth Landing

Apollo of the plague
gifts hexameter to
foreign-tongued Sybil
chanting from her rock

His laurel hut
hidden in dense woods
a toad
under a root

it seems the lynx
is only visible
if she cares to be
nonchalant before the kill

a sorceress fed by prophecy and bees
lighting the logos
in the space between
the photon and the place where it had been

earth from earth
back from moon
no longer earth
to land upon

Fondamenta degli Incurabili

the passing of light
in opulence
over her back
turned into grass

the sheen of white
then mint green leaves
twist into limbs
of olive boughs

when ripe fruit flesh
is pulled apart
her secret self
is made overt

Domestic rain

the ceiling leaked
on to the shelf
the Shelley book
curled like a shell

because, never mind
lawnmowers and
local songbirds
and leaf-blowers

Hic et nusquam

Here and not here
nowhere on the flight
path leading through
the wooded end of the estate
scholars walk behind the trees
heads bowed
Here and nowhere as a motto
of our endless search to leave
behind a name and history
apocryphal stories of my father
mythic London and the Middle East
grief the shape of
one drowned child
face down so easily
what are we left standing with
holding a coat with tiny sleeves
every detail travels across space
to be here exactly for no purpose

who fucks the mother in the grass
travelling salesman (no such thing these days)
who wades between her sheets
hung out to dry
smelling air caught in the breeze
between striped flannel. Docents in the square
point anywhere as children jostle for the aftermath parade
I'm lost to any cause lost to any treaty I agreed to make

A Piacere

Blood hosed down
the paving slabs
my sink stand sways
sliced fish gills on
the marble chopping block
Riot police
washed away like
a mistake
you get annoyed
at my desire
reduces you you say
in the world's view
it is my needs as much
as violence
torpedoing the Halifax
in her caesura
too bad Bella
moved to Germany
floodlit street in curfew
tangerine and aqua blue
moths and cops
come out of nowhere
for the show
the flares smell so familiar
the screams subside
across the square
untended candles
keep a vigil after
all the people go

Ephemera

What helps it man that the stars and the waters gleam?
—Swinburne

Brassy-pewter flash
as slow worm parts its path
casting a tiny umber shade
between its body and the earth
as mayfly down the river
landing incidentally
(alive only a day)
and later green drake flies
(alive for two days)
on the River Dee
or Wye

Consuming chaos

neither a boat nor a body seem-
ingly heading downstream

thought turned to fear
as soul dissolves in shower

the fealty of selfhood
swaying overboard

an eager corpse
for an endless sea

others abated others contained
others released of themselves

a snake that swallows
a swallow that swallows a snake

the sea and the land rush together
the last loaf of bread has been baked

we will crawl on our hands and knees
as we search for a last place to sleep

we collapse in ignorance there
as the shore unfolds and unfolds

Golden Satellite Debris

The horizontal night is innocent
of need—a grid invisible
the universe
I disappear into
the town
spread infinite below
vertical for years
I look down now
there is no centre there
the world is nowhere near

the tiny girl who drew a map
of life chose blue and yellow

Golden satellite debris
formally collected for
Sister Agatha etc.

saints stand on parapets
meals of sweet peppers
raisins and tongue
stain the railings
rain keeps raining on

grief follows the sun
down to complete
the horizon
the girl I see
playing knows
nothing of me
her life an instant
the night quite empty

even a cloud eventually
opens out its identity
we see a rabbit then a goat
on our way for tea & toast

the barn owl flies over
the orchard dusk
the field gone to seed
the plough turned to rust

On Maluerne Hill
I read a sumer season
step off into
May's oblivion

each book an
abandoned villa
sage tweed hillock
folded over

the wild pear grew
for 3 centuries
until we cut it down
for the new railway

On reflection

look at the river
from the bridge
I see a face
foreign to me

I wake too late
to clarify the dream
I half recall uncertainty
uncertainly again

below I see
the steady stream
a yellow maple leaf
floats over me

a series of green canvasses
muted gold and Aztec blue
glazing the abyss
draining the essential

he painted in a garden shed
abandoned them unfinished
said he'd had enough of this
leapt off a balcony. Is dead

we are the sort of people
we were warned about
wandering the Maquis
void of true intent

a country of gypsies
mountebanks and whores
tumbling for a living
falling without cause

metal from the tip
metal from the tip
rustier the better
buried in a skip

une valise énorme
filled with paper scraps
a life made up of notes
left at someone's flat

a temple to Mercury
erected in haste
made out of a dead walnut tree
and household waste

the white-smocked girls march
to mark the date
their short-haired martyr Joan
was burned at the stake

Utopian saltworks
on noxious slums
Verdun ossuaries
frogs and huns

cuckoo duplicity
feast of worms
reed warbler protestations
sung in twenty bursts

brambling, linnet
shrike or thrush
a mighty golden fortress
made of straw & grass

The leaves make the face
of Simone de Beauvoir
a beautiful sight
the breeze disappears

Lay about Marie
bright as the sun
Lay sung in silence
Just for no-one

Lay about Piers
Dead in her arms
Died in the field
Fell for her charms

Layabout poet
Waking too late
Dreamt of a fighter plane
Crashed in the lake

Late English summer
Changeable skies
Rhubarb in flower
Diamonds and flies

Gorgeous red clusters
Gleaming like wounds
Cheese in the larder
Starting to bloom

She walks with a cane
She laughs with a wheeze
She sleeps with a leopard
Skin rug on her knees

The dust covers the earth
Glistering like gold
A child goes to her grave
Sooner than she should

A farmer cut her head off
Stored it in some milk
The village put it in the sky
Wrapped in golden silk

Earth made of earth
Song made of air
When the earth is buried
Who will sing thereof

The feet of the Buddha
are covered by water
the Yangtze river
rising in winter

Jaipur city
shakes like thunder
until the lake
appears to fill

wake up when
the ceiling falls
a pink earthquake
of waste and swill

Worcestershire murder

her body underneath the hedge
her legs stick out into the lane
her torso floating in the lake
at night making an obscure shape.

Summer school

Today the lawns of Trinity combust
otherwise
we could have stayed outside
to play croquet

The erstwhile gods

It has been suggested that the body (soma) is the tomb (sema) for the soul, that the sign (sema) written over our corpse is the only adventure of our lives. This story, a fragmentary one at best, is the tale the gods tell themselves, gods being words (logos), and myth the occasions of their telling. Whether we understand or even believe in our role is unimportant, the gods will play through us as a tune plays through the aulos, arousing many thoughts and feelings but never leading us any closer to our undisclosed purpose.

The grass trembles: Apollo
sings his season change
the wind rails round the house
the grass thrills under snow

The Beloved (Adonis)

So scared so young
he hasn't had a proper hard-on yet
out here in the wild dark
he knows that god
will rescue him
a transformation
that consumes his life

The gods return not
as a remedy but as a riot
for evolution requires a
revolution bursting
leaf-like over our heads
Youth was always the arena
where the gods announced desires
the shape of one young breast
hung as the scooter passes
a Molotov spreads across the grease
y boulevard the barricades
of café chairs and bistro stools
gods dagger through the sirens
and the panicked city beasts

Thanatos

I was afraid after
After I lost mother

When my father died
We became the same person

Leaving me a view of half the world
above me half below

Soft secrets held away from us
When did we forget such things as happiness

Babel

From night to softest dawn
slowly words awoke
the fragile earth
an artichoke
dangerous and still.

ants move spheres of clay
to build a giant hill
from night to day
across the gley
until it broke

Roma

Ruins bear witness to this: that the past is not there.
—Roberto Calasso

City of cats and
the murdered Remus
Tivoli's interiors
now open to the elements

when all the gods attend
the gala performance
we have a chance to purchase
postcard monuments

City of cats and
dented cars
cafés where
murdered Remus sat

secular tourists
wander without
exposed interiors
foundations of faith

having worked
having stopped
Palinurus
stepped off

Hermes

The swamp-green typewriter
intelligent to touch
vain, beautiful, light

as a feather
swifter than
a thought

Joy has run dry
the docks no longer
build a boat
convincingly

long since the poet
sailed this way
past green-haired nymphs
heralding ecstasy

(Hekate)

The dark red night opens her luscious mouth
And yawns her tiny rabbit tongue in half
They curl for hours in partial light
A question mark that's answered before dawn

Friday oysters (Aphrodite)

We clamber blind
into the chamber hall
inside the hidden cochlea

A vessel pouring dreams
over an ocean floor
where desire coils in a shell

Ecstasy falls
into fleshy wounds
tongues that are sister to the touch

tugging at cherry pits
bitten by pearly teeth
swallow a briny gulp

Narcissus

Gorgeously drowned
The deer floats by
Four legs up like
A table upside down
The flooded church
With ringing bell
A solo duet echoing
Echoing the dale
Can there be another voice
Underneath my song
The pristine lake
Sings into the well

Daphne

Daphne turned into a hare
then a leaf then a tree
then a coward then a warrior
all of it fear, all of it ecstasy

Rain slows
into a water ache
wind bends grass
like a mourner's neck

somewhere in memory
dogs howl in misery

hopeless with
agony

Immortal fuck
indifferent to suffering

A god is named
a conquerer king

Watching a spider arm
intricating a web

Watching the background blur
soft as a water bear

None of the sorrow lost
none of the anger lasts

Water drips finally
rejoining water

Burning Saturday all day for satyrs
tied my hands behind your back
the rain which comes at last
pissing on the evening's dark morass

Wine/Maenad

Her soul-pearls drip
into the ruby cave
we cannot move until
another crashing wave

grief spurts in the bath
grief spills in the glass
a rosy glow spreads out
as sun ripens her face

Snail-Aphrodite

into the smallest shell
the crab has crawled

that there is a heaven
hidden here on earth

Sulis Minerva

a sparkly head
with grass and yeast
y champagne
in the wooz
y a-tri-um

Selene

The eggmoon was a head we could not see
fall past earth in silent vulnerability
frozen in its secret canister
it was a dreaming passenger
her face asleep against the glass

Alectrona

Beauty clothes the egg with flame
a yielding yellow bridal gown

Thanatos

Fresh mercenaries pluck the fruit
from orchards derelict behind
abandoned farms and abattoirs
the concrete stained rust-brown with blood

Pontus

The sea was abandoned
Just up against the land
We wandered closer in
From its elastic hand

With tiny knots we fidgeted
A massacred world
A complex mess of brilliance
burnt across the veldt

The sea came back into our lives
As if a special memory
Had risen up to claim once more
Its preeminent ancestry

Eros

fickle boy this morrow
terrified and bored
waits for love to sooth
his tautened bow

love's pierced heart
warming by the fire
tears our future
happiness apart

Dis Pater

green houses
whose blind eyes
shatter under
lunar winds

Æther-Orpheus

That the gods are dead or like the dead
And cannot be directly spoken to

Only with words that are thrown away
Only when we are forgotten

Can words pass between these alien realms
homeless in their passion.

*

seven strings seven vowels seven circles of heaven
Orpheus flies around the globe with the names of the gods he is given

Of Plato's Cave

We might read Plato's cave as the body: the lowly consuming bowels of the animal, the stomach, up to the loftier heart giving truth to highest of all the knowing senses that vent through the throat's voice—the cave's tunnel, passage of the escaping breath of the psyche—releasing the body out into the logos, pure realm of knowledge and divine unity.

Delphinus

That spirit once escaped
for thirty thousand years
circling the earth
Contained in wood and flesh

Always on the brink
Forgetful and forgotten
The dolphin's endless dive
Into the wave receding

Mercury

Dream of an often-shifting house
        walls made of wind, windows of ice
            home to the swift
                    landing on emptiness

Song

Just as blind Orpheus leads us on
to his final resting place
a song where only ghosts remain
a bolt that smells of lavender and ash

here by the roots here in a wooded dell
What of the living being
What of the passing sense
Where in the past is found
mourning this final scene

Prayer

When we ask the gods
for a particular
wavelength of a certain colour
in muddy water

objects of love
discarded by lovers
the subject of death
the morning after

Two octaves for Octavius

A spider's web
To hang herself
A bat whose son
Is ripped apart
The gods do not
Forgive a slight
A creature flies
In sacrifice

When the cat dies
We're not certain
Which of us died
Which carries on
The world's piano
Plays its tune
Note after note
Is soon forgotten

Demeter eats the pink prawns without sauce, shell and tentacles whole. She likes the crunch and soft meat contrast in her mouth. Sara likes the spears of asparagus in hollandaise, whereas Damita eats boiled eggs with salt and pepper on a wholewheat cracker with her tea.

In the centre of the agora the urchins dry. Flames made of marble decorate the doorway to the cellar where the mushrooms wait. A shiver that starts in the spine and works throughout the senses sends the town near blind. She is looking for her daughter in the underworld.

We do not want to kiss the goddess as she doesn't wash her mouth, a scent of dirt and offal from her eyes and ears, her dress wafts by smelly of the farmyard and we burst alive. Her throat is like a Dutch canal, her stomach grinds the seashells in a rock pool swell. Six bells from the ankles mark her trail.

Bacchus

The climate bomb drops
on the grasses and the frogs
as the amputees fuck on the beach

The nighttime is done
with laughter and less
as we open the door to the car

I've given up drinking
until the next drink
and loving until I can love

Without one another
we run for the cover
of fashionable decorative books

I've written my memoir
to read in the mirror
it rhymes with itself for a while

To put down the answer
in captions and headings
I've used up my time turn the page

I smile at the waitress
who's here as my witness
and swallows my pride and my rage

cheerio sister jesus cheerio madame rizla bon voyage missy judas
      and Frank
I'll call in the morning from over the mountain
where the vineyards smoulder in ranks

The Red Book

The red book

Work on that one
said the poet in my dream
what I wanted was
to travel to a foreign place familiar-

ly unravelling for once
the always absent other
and the almost willing loss
opening the kitchen door

to someone else's kitchen
not unlike my own
or walking down
some white stone steps

pots of lavender with bees
pots of gauche geraniums
poets of this empty scene
and other once-elysiums

under the strange-rooted trees
the tree roots share details
of me passing overhead
an alien moon flower

the bees don't seem to bother
reckoning the truth
Here is the last night
of their last summer.

What we as ancestors have left is
poisonous cities
and a near total collapse
of all moralities

wealthier than god we
stay in bed to shit
the pigeons in the loft
turn snapshots into paste

something both disgusting
and appropriate to the lost
fantasy of legacy:
Despair's uplifting hope

searching for a red hut
to call our home
went over to the neighbours
with a bottle of red wine
ready to replace our guilt
with crimson-robed abandonment.

The red hut shivered
underneath a spruce
I don't want to have to
keep rehearsing this:

Red hut, wet shoes,
green sky, red clouds
I'd rather it had stayed unsaid
I'd rather I'd stayed at home.

Last night giant shapes
passed each other in the dark
this morning when I wake

feeling something like an aftershock
(strangers nearly kissing in the park
we can't quite figure out
where we know each other from)
waking in a foreign bed
unfamiliar window frame
the sunlit curtains amber edged with red
an exhibition poster on the kitchen wall
(the flesh tones have all faded blue)
Caravaggio's *Boy bitten by a lizard*
has no business being thus depicted
in a painting as the god of wine
too young too desirable too dead

The fires of California choke the sky
he is dying and we have little left to say
I make another cup of Yorkshire tea
try to read *Stendhal* but still can't

An orange light comes through the blinds
this means the air is awful and the day
outside smells of bonfire and inside
a sweet blue odor settles in the throat.

The salamander symbolizes fire
like other snakes it wants to die
gripped in the painter's hand
under his ruby lips

dark and red the cherries plucked
deathly green leaf shadows frame
pink desirous peonies
hidden in the foliage
the tiny serpent mouth aflame
with nothing left to say

Bacchus looking terrified
outside the gallery
outside the poem
where the fuck are we
now in California
Michelangelo Merisi de Caravaggio
Eros with his leg hitched up
(Bacchus and Eros are identical)
Holofernes and Goliath
(giants with their heads cut off)
enormous redwoods
rows of vines
what do these shadows indicate
it's such a tiny snake
outside the scullery
where in the hell am I
animals now running by
while I was sitting here
Le Rouge et le Noir unread
what are they running from
where are they running to

*

The eyes replaced by red
The trees also by red
The animals that fled the flames
They were replaced by red

In a Foreign Country

World moves away from us
        Christopher Swan
Where are you swimming to?
        And what upon?

The moon lays fabric
over the sea
over the sleepers
drifting from land.

*

All the planes drop from the sky,
are we beautiful because disinterested?
A former lover wanders by
blows a kiss without knowing it

*

I had thought
London was a solid
object but
it was a liquid

*

Hope and tomorrow
crawled into shadow
The dove and the lion
asleep in the meadow

The silver green berries
of juniper bushes
scattered like trash
amidst all the ashes

The cry of an owl
The cry of a child
The groan of a word
dry in a field

*

My poisoned eye
dreams of a green
the æther-face
of Queen Aurora

Dear flower
I don't even
in whose garden
I no longer

Dear River
can't either
hidden underneath
forever

Dear Leaves
Dead leaves
So beautiful and golden
I mean forgotten

What the world wants
never clear
We are the corpse flower
in the newspaper

pouring out odour
reeking with pleasure
over the mountain over the forest
over the noise of the molested future

*

Hearing the swallows
I thought were angels
maybe devils
they were neither

Hearing their bugles
skimming the valley
I was the victim
and the invader

*

Fascist5 children
move in a swarm
convene in my head
converge in my room

*

Winter culvert
Brackish skies
metal workers
galvanized

Frozen windows
rotten lungs
factory workforce
downsized

*

If I take the kayak
wandering downstream
forgetting who I am
someone will take aim

We all count to zero
breathing through a mask
In acidic light
trying to relax

hoping to forgive
myself for being
whoever this
stranger is.

*

I say I'm in a garden
it obviously can't be true
a garden filled with
the roses were removed.

There are hundreds of birds   in the garden
and photons that land   on their wings
the leaves are the colour   they're singing
whose silence remains in the trees

you know each detail makes this
just as it disappears
the garden is filled with songs
and echoes nobody hears.

*

The universe
descends on us
in silver dust

we notice as
the light walks past
a collared dove

In ualle lacrimarum

Inside the CIA's
secret Kabul base
burned out and
abandoned in haste

The faux Afghani village where
they trained paramilitary forces
linked to some of the worst
human rights abuses

How to escape America

The light is everywhere
she eats a lobster claw
the Baptist church burns down
we dance a Charleston
laughing in the rain etc.
at the crash the passenger
is not yet dead
having given head
the cables spark across the road
the light pours down
domestic staff walk home
past Halloween displays
lit up inflated Santa Claus
and well-fed dogs
complaining to their neighbours
as the grouse dash under
flood lit work discounted stores
post no bills accessories
latin quarter NYC
apologize for the delay
flood lit bridge
first month free
foreign money news on CNN
orthodox jew tenements
ten commandments
in the middle of the street
dancer freaking out
I've got no right
You've got no right
trepidation as the door opens
The October Sale
union strike
asteroid strike

on the Yucatan
we still don't know
how to better understand
the largest living organism
is not a honey mushroom
pando aspen saltwater
crocodile oil tanker
misinformation regarding drinking water

    *

Above if underneath the sky
and deep within the rivers swam
aquatic living souls like deities
a realm that is not useless before sin
but joyous cultivation
the body of a living man or dead
four rivers are four humours
fructifying the eternal seed
sliding towards Jericho
the bandits meeting on the road
we had exited paradise
of our own accord
greeting the devil in our deed
no need to steal what you have grown
the seed already in the apple
no animal was made to leave

    *

the headless corpse you squeeze
and fondle is your own
blood stains the dashboard
and covers all the crowd
dying in their seats—

a shroud the size of the United States
dyed indigo and red
w/ 50 star-shaped puncture wounds
falls across our vision of escape
Heaven's sewn into the seam
but can't be read—instead
we shout to hear ourselves perform sincerity
lost before the ensign was spread out

When England last in the door jar jammed

When England last in the door jar jammed
We were at war with ignorance
The prams were herded in the hall
And all bemoaned the dance of Death.

When nightjars last in the doorjamb flew
Who was then the gentleman?
After you, no after you!
And all who saw him said amen.

Pastoral invasion

The swallow-pilgrims whistle all
around the village green
tanks rumble past most joyously
before the rural scene

an antiaircraft gun
pointing at the clock
waits until it's noon
to detonate its shock

we shall have lemon cake for tea
sachertorte & petits fours
the colonel is invited in despite
the orphans' well-established fears

afterwards it's winter
before the summer fête
the leaves will drop on top of all those
buried in the street

strewn across the graves
poppies and primroses
sherry and advocaat
the crowd dispersed with hoses

O where have all the swallows
gone across the fields and tundra
we sit alone and wait for one
to signal it is summer

*

The bees fly over the crimson
carmine, puce and mauve
the envelope of manilla
arrives at 11 o'clock

The muse suckles Jesus
the muse suckles geese
she suckles a phalanx of soldiers
the roses, the daisies, the ghosts:

I wanted to be the bees
I wanted to be the geese
to live a life of having sex
with everything I meet.

*

Over the farms and the fiddlehead ferns
over the plastic waste
a large black bird I don't recognize
flies to an unknown place

In a Foreign Country

If I lie down now
in the undergrowth

a railway bank
near Fernhill Heath

it is only for a while
for a short rest

in the crunching brack
and thappy mulch

a single hour
to recuperate somehow

between what was my home
and the departing train

a short stay just
a shallow nest

a rest, an hour, a day
until I am quite ready

to return again
to a foreign country

Shahed-136

The witnesses fly over fields
over the schools & cement slabs
The mopeds drone over the trees
& hospital cemeteries

Shepherds release their flocks
teachers burn their books
a nurse poisons the drinking well
as witnesses collapse.

Spring '71

A stream runs through the house
freezing on the kitchen tiles
huddled round the parlor fire
we dream of polar bears and killer whales

Christmas '76

Voilà emptiness
voilà silver foil
ornamentals for
our one true festival

Vinylsingle

In the blurry polaroid the eyes are red
glass beads decorating Christmas trees
happily still working class
45 revs on the portable dansette

Super8

the chromium girls whirr as the reel ends
golden afternoon globes hover in the reeds
his smile erupts and is repeated endlessly
tomorrow is a kingdom we shall never see

Afterword

Golden Satellite Debris is my 13th book. I don't feel particularly superstitious about that. I do still feel as if a book of mine coming into the world is unprecedented, a mix of hope and failure. What am I trying to do? At least, I think, I am trying to write with a kind of joy and grace a lyric that somehow manages to be both strange and familiar. The poems almost always start with a phrase, an announced phrase that seems to require me to echo and support it. In this regard, my poems are not ever really just mine. They might contain biographical aspects, but they are just as likely to contain flashes of lives that have never existed anywhere else as far as I know. They are certainly shaped by contemporary concerns, forest fires in California (I live one state over in Idaho, and we often see the effects in our smog and our sunsets), wars wherever they are now happening, natural and unnatural disasters. There is perhaps a pervasive atmosphere of loss and sadness. Maybe even of melancholy. Some of that seems to be the fault of the poet. Equally, much of it seems to be a response to the world we now live in. Neither can escape the other.

And so the one question I might ask myself is what is a book of poems doing in this day and age? And I might answer, the same as it ever was. If I feel hopeless at times, it is not that I feel art or poetry has lost its purpose. It might be that it is more necessary than ever. And not as an escape, not as a little game played by a lucky, educated few, sat aside from the major catastrophes of the world (though that could be someone else's description of what takes place). I see poetry as being tasked with unveiling new realities, even in its play and its apparent whimsy. Poetry brings to our attention a unique and quavering glory of being, a sense of the self as a curious thing made and making. If the common concerns of the world these days are materialistic, even capitalistic, or rampantly technological, it is necessary for these to take their place in a confabulation of possibilities. The human condition ought not to be described in such limited ways. Language, the great creative tool of the Homo Sapiens, is not a servant to such things. It is not a tool merely to execute plans of consumption and competition. It is a realm also of joy and excess and possibility. It can be used to remind us of the infinite scope of love and pleasure, even as, and because, it describes and acknowledges sadness and loss.

Surely the world is still glorious. Surely life is? If we are tired of the world, or tired of being human we can also see that that is only a phase in the sequences of possibilities. Poems are complicated glimpses of never complete worlds. They are an ancient technology, an almost atemporal projection of absence and presence that allows us to imagine and accept the glories and agonies of being. That sounds like a lot to put on a few lines of reproduced type, but it is surely what we might put on any moment of any day (every moment of everyday if we had the energy and will to do so).

The title points towards a sense of the wonder and glory of life on this planet, the *Golden* (with a hint of the sun setting no doubt), but also a sense of life as an aftermath, *Debris*, a sort of arbitrary and accidental outcome of equations and collisions only some of which we are aware of. I see the earth as a *Satellite*, a contingent object moving in space, but on a smaller scale also the human and the poem, spinning around some unknown centre, whether we call that truth, being, love or death.

MARTIN CORLESS-SMITH

www.ingramcontent.com/pod-product-compliance
Lightning Source LLC
Chambersburg PA
CBHW031634160426
43196CB00006B/419